RUTH BADER GINSBURG

Supreme Court Justice

— PEOPLE TO KNOW —

RUTH BADER GINSBURG
Supreme Court Justice

Carmen Bredeson

ENSLOW PUBLISHERS, INC.

44 Fadem Road
Box 699
Springfield, N.J. 07081
U.S.A.

P.O. Box 38
Aldershot
Hants GU12 6BP
U.K.

Library of Congress Cataloging-in-Publication Data

Bredeson, Carmen.
    Ruth Bader Ginsburg: Supreme Court justice / Carmen Bredeson.
        p. cm. — (People to know)
    Includes bibliographical references and index.
    ISBN 0-89490-621-6
    1. Ginsburg, Ruth Bader—Juvenile literature. 2. Judges—United
States—Biography—Juvenile literature. I. Title. II. Series.
KF8745.G56B74 1995
347.73'2634—dc20
[B]
[347.3073534]   95-12286
[B]   CIP

Printed in the United States of America

10 9 8 7 6 5 4 3 2 1

Illustration Credits: Collection of the Supreme Court of the United States,
pp. 14, 16, 18, 20, 23, 30, 38, 51, 62, 78, 80, 94, 112; Franz Jantzen,
Collection of the Supreme Court of the United States, pp. 82, 84, 89, 101;
©Smithsonian Institution, p. 6; ©The National Geographic Society,
courtesy of The Supreme Court Historical Society, p. 92; The White
House, p. 76.

Cover Illustration: ©The National Geographic Society, courtesy of The
Supreme Court Historical Society

Contents

Ruth Bader Ginsburg

Nomination to the Supreme Court

The United States Supreme Court ruled in an 1873 case that it was legal to prevent a woman from practicing law. In *Bradwell* v. *Illinois*, the highest court in the land said: "The paramount destiny and mission of [women] are to fulfill the noble and benign offices of wife and mother. This is the law of the Creator."[1]

One hundred twenty years later, in 1993, Judge Ruth Bader Ginsburg appeared before a gathering of family and friends in the Rose Garden of the White House in Washington, D.C. She stood quietly by the side of President Bill Clinton and listened as he said:

> Article 2, Section 2 of the United States Constitution empowers the President to select a nominee to fill a vacancy on the Supreme Court of the United States. This responsibility is one of the most significant duties assigned to the President by the Constitution.[2]

President Clinton then nominated Federal Circuit Court Judge Ruth Bader Ginsburg to be the 107th Justice of the Supreme Court. If confirmed by the Senate, she would be only the second woman named to the High Court in the history of the United States. Judge Ginsburg would replace retiring Justice Byron White, who had been a member of the Supreme Court since 1962. Supreme Court Justices are appointed for life or until they choose to retire. They do not rise and fall with the political parties that are in office but remain on the bench throughout the changes that take place in the federal administration. In his introductory remarks about Judge Ruth Bader Ginsburg, Clinton said:

> . . . in her years on the bench she has genuinely distinguished herself as one of our nation's best judges: progressive in outlook, wise in judgment, balanced and fair in her opinions. . . . Over the course of a lifetime, in her pioneering work on behalf of the women of this country, she has compiled a truly historic record of achievement in the finest traditions of American law and citizenship.[3]

As the President went on to describe her early life and career, Judge Ginsburg gazed into the audience. The bright June sunshine reflected in her sparkling eyes and intensified the color of her royal blue suit. Ginsburg appeared to be having a wonderful time. Her lovely smile got wider and wider as she found the familiar faces of the family and friends who were seated before her.

Ruth Bader Ginsburg's life seemed perfect on that beautiful June day, but there had been many difficult events in her past that had helped shape her character.

During her teenage years, Ruth Bader watched as her mother, Celia Bader, slowly lost a battle with cancer. Celia Bader died in 1950, on the eve of Ruth's high school graduation. Soon after Ruth Bader's marriage to Martin Ginsburg in 1954, he too developed an often-fatal form of cancer. His illness was very serious, but he managed to survive the ordeal. In 1993, Ruth and Martin Ginsburg had been married for thirty-nine years. They were the parents of a son and a daughter and the grandparents of a granddaughter and a grandson.

When Ruth Bader Ginsburg entered Harvard Law School in 1956, she was one of only nine women enrolled in a class of 500. Despite some very tough competition, she was chosen for the *Law Review* staff, an honor that was reserved for the top students. Ginsburg transferred to Columbia Law School in 1958, again made *Law Review*, and graduated in a tie for first place in the class of 1959.

In spite of her excellent academic record, Ginsburg could not find a job after graduation. She interviewed at several law firms, but not one of them called back to offer the new attorney a position. She said later, "A woman, a Jew, and a mother. Three strikes. It was too much."[4]

In his introduction of Ruth Bader Ginsburg, President Clinton said:

> Having experienced discrimination, she devoted the next 20 years of her career to fighting it and making this country a better place for our wives, our mothers, our sisters and our daughters. She argued and won many of the women's rights cases before the Supreme Court in the 1970s. Many admirers of her work say she is to the women's movement what former Supreme Court Justice Thurgood Marshall was to the movement for the rights of African-Americans.[5]

In addition to her work on behalf of gender equality, Ruth Bader Ginsburg had served for the past thirteen years as a judge on the United States Court of Appeals for the District of Columbia Circuit. (These courts of appeals are the second-highest courts in the land.)

Over the door of the main entrance to the Supreme Court building in Washington, D.C., are the words "Equal Justice Under Law." Even though the Constitution of the United States proclaimed equal Justice for all, that had not been the case for women in the United States. In the past, women were often treated as second-class citizens. They were not even permitted to vote in most states or hold public office until 1920.

Women had staged a courageous battle in their fight for equality. Even though a great deal of progress had been made, there was still a long way to go when Ruth Bader Ginsburg took up the fight in the 1970s. She argued six landmark cases before the Supreme Court and won five of them. Those cases helped to establish the precedents that eventually eliminated some of the laws that treated men and women differently.

Ginsburg's list of accomplishments also included being the first female tenured law professor at Columbia University. She was not the first female Supreme Court Justice, though. That honor went to Justice Sandra Day O'Connor, who was appointed by President Ronald Reagan in 1981. Ruth Bader Ginsburg's appointment would nonetheless be historic. If confirmed, she would be only the second woman to serve on the Supreme Court in its 203-year history.

After President Clinton concluded his remarks, Ginsburg smiled, stepped to the podium, and said, "Mr. President, I am grateful beyond measure for the confidence you have placed in me, and I will strive, with all that I have, to live up to your expectations in making this appointment."[6] She then spoke briefly about the advances that women had made in the legal profession during the past twenty years.

Next, Ginsburg introduced her husband, Martin Ginsburg, their son, James, and their son-in-law, George T. Spera, Jr. Their daughter, Jane Ginsburg, could not be present for the ceremony but called her mother to say good luck. Ruth Bader Ginsburg related that in Jane's 1973 high school yearbook, listed under ambition, was the desire to see her mother appointed to the Supreme

Court. "The next line read: If necessary, Jane will appoint her. Jane is so pleased, Mr. President, that you did it instead, and her brother, James, is, too."[7]

Ginsburg smiled as she thanked her husband, Martin, and all of the members of her family who had offered support and encouragement throughout her career. She said:

> I have been aided by my life's partner, Martin D. Ginsburg, who has been since our teenage years my best friend and biggest booster; by my mother-in-law, Evelyn Ginsburg, the most supportive parent a person could have; and by a daughter and son with the taste to appreciate that Daddy cooks ever so much better than Mommy—and so phased me out of the kitchen at a relatively early age.[8]

As her remarks came to a close, Ruth Bader Ginsburg said:

> I have a last thank-you. It is to my mother, Celia Amster Bader, the bravest and strongest person I have known, who was taken from me much too soon. I pray that I may be all that she would have been, had she lived in an age when women could aspire and achieve, and daughters are cherished as much as sons.[9]

2

Early Years

Ruth Bader was born in Brooklyn, New York, on March 15, 1933, and lived in a neighborhood called Flatbush. Her parents, Celia and Nathan Bader, also had another daughter. Marilyn was five years old when baby Ruth was born. When Ruth was just one year old, her big sister Marilyn contracted meningitis, a serious infection of the spinal cord and brain. The disease led to Marilyn's tragic death at the age of six. After Marilyn died, Celia Bader lavished all of her considerable attention on her remaining daughter, Ruth.

Ruth's mother, Celia Amster Bader, was the daughter of immigrants who came to America from central Europe. She graduated from high school when she was just fifteen years old but was not able to continue her education. Instead, Celia had to go to work

Ruth Bader, age two, was born in Brooklyn, New York.

so that her older brother, Solomon, could attend college. Her love of learning never diminished though, and she spent hours every day reading to her little daughter, Ruth.

Celia Bader would often rush through her household chores early in the day. With something left simmering in the stew pot on the stove, mother and daughter would escape to the library and spend the afternoon lost in a world of books. The library that they visited was located over a Chinese restaurant. Later in her life, Ruth Ginsburg would say that ever since her childhood "she has associated the aroma of Chinese food with the pleasures of reading."[1]

The afternoon hours passed quickly for Ruth and her mother, as they worked their way through piles of books. When dinnertime approached, they would put their library books away and return home to greet Ruth's father, Nathan Bader. He owned and operated a small clothing store in the Flatbush neighborhood.

In addition to her afternoons in the library, Ruth had her cousin, Richard Bader, as a companion. Born just three months apart, Ruth and Richard lived in the same house until they were four years old. The family was somewhat unusual because the children's mothers were sisters and their fathers were brothers. Until his death in 1989, Richard Bader and Ruth Bader Ginsburg remained very close.[2]

Ruth attended Brooklyn P. S. (Public School) 238 during her elementary school years, and she sometimes

Ruth was three months younger than her cousin, Richard Bader.

went to camp in the summer. During her childhood, she was often called Kiki, a name that was given to her when she was just a baby by her sister Marilyn.

After elementary school, Ruth went on to James Madison High School in Brooklyn. She made excellent grades there and was a member of Arista, which was an academic honor society. She also served as the editor of the school newspaper, *The Highway Herald.* While she was on the newspaper staff, Ruth wrote two editorials that examined the meaning of the United States Constitution's Bill of Rights and the Magna Carta. The Magna Carta was signed by King John in England in 1215. The charter helped establish a more constitutional form of government in which individual rights were protected. Even in high school, Ruth Bader was beginning to be interested in law.

Ruth also participated in many extracurricular activities at Madison High School. As a member of the pep squad, she and her fellow cheerleaders were called "Go-Getters." They wore black satin jackets and sold football tickets before the games. Ruth was also a baton twirler and played the cello in the school band. She was an active and popular student, and she somehow managed to keep her life at school and her life at home separate. Ruth Bader almost never talked to her friends about the tragic situation that she faced every day when she got home from school.

Cousins Ruth and Richard Bader were close friends.

Her mother, Celia Bader, was diagnosed with cervical cancer when Ruth was in the ninth grade. Throughout Ruth's high school years, Celia Bader's health deteriorated a little more with each passing month. When she arrived home from school, Ruth often went to her mother's room and sat by the bed while she did her homework. During her senior year, Ruth spent many of her free hours next to her dying mother's bed. The night before Ruth's high school graduation, Celia Bader finally lost her long battle with cancer and died at the age of forty-seven. Ruth did not attend graduation, and her various awards were delivered to her house by some of the teachers from James Madison High School.

Through the years, Celia Bader had managed to save $5,000. The money was to be used for Ruth's college education. Celia's own dream of a college degree was never realized, but she was determined that her daughter would have an opportunity to further her education. As it turned out, Ruth did not need the money. Her performance and grades in high school had been excellent. She was awarded several scholarships that helped pay for her years at Cornell University, located in Ithaca, New York.

Ruth Bader enrolled at Cornell in the fall of 1950. She worked hard and was a good student, but she later said, "There was a problem with Cornell in the '50s . . . . The most important degree for you to get was Mrs., and it didn't do to be seen reading and studying." She added,

Ruth Bader, age fifteen, attended James Madison High School in Brooklyn, New York.

"I knew some pretty obscure libraries on the Cornell campus." During her years at Cornell, "the thing to do was to be a party girl. It's long gone, but it was the tone of the '50s."[3]

It was during her freshmen year that Ruth Bader met Martin Ginsburg, a sophomore who was majoring in chemistry. Martin Ginsburg, the son of wealthy parents, was an avid golfer and had a very outgoing personality. The couple dated for the next three years and became engaged during Bader's junior year. It was while she was at Cornell that Ruth Bader first thought about studying law.

Ruth Bader took several government courses and worked as a research assistant for Professor Robert Cushman. During their association, Cushman often expressed his views concerning the importance of the rights of freedom of speech, thought, and the press. He had no tolerance for anyone who would threaten those basic rights, and he praised attorneys who tried to protect them. Ruth Bader Ginsburg later said about those experiences at Cornell:

> That a lawyer could do something that was personally satisfying and at the same time work to preserve the values that have made this country great was an exciting prospect for me.[4]

Ruth Bader talked to her father about her decision to study law. He questioned whether she could support herself as an attorney. Her father suggested that a teaching certificate might be a more practical choice. In the 1950s, there were very few women attorneys employed in the United States.

In 1954, Ruth Bader graduated with high honors and a bachelor of arts degree in government from Cornell University. Martin Ginsburg had graduated from Cornell the year before and had just completed has first year at Harvard Law School in Cambridge, Massachusetts.

On June 23, 1954, Ruth Bader and Martin Ginsburg were married. Before the young couple could settle down into their new life, Martin Ginsburg was drafted into the armed services. He was sent to Fort Sill in Lawton, Oklahoma, for training and active duty. In 1954, all men in the United States who were over the age of eighteen were expected to serve two years of active duty in the military.

After the Ginsburgs were settled in Oklahoma, Ruth found a job in the local Social Security office, where she worked as a clerk typist. It was there, in her government job, that Ruth Bader Ginsburg faced gender discrimination for the first time. When she was hired to work in the Social Security office, she was given a GS-5 employee rating. In order to learn more about the job, Ginsburg was scheduled to attend a training session in Baltimore, Maryland.

Just before the session began, Ruth and Martin Ginsburg learned that they would be parents for the first time. When Ruth Ginsburg's boss found out that she was

Martin Ginsburg and Ruth Bader were married on June 23, 1954.

pregnant, her extra training sessions were cancelled. She was also demoted to a GS-2 position that earned much lower wages. At that time, pregnancy was often viewed as a condition that required extra rest and very little physical activity. Ginsburg accepted her fate and did not attempt to reverse the decision. In the 1950s, women rarely protested unequal treatment in the workplace.

Ruth Bader Ginsburg continued to work in the Social Security office until the birth of Jane on July 21, 1955. Shortly after the baby's birth, Martin Ginsburg's term in the service was completed. The family returned to Cambridge, Massachusetts, so Martin Ginsburg could resume his law school education at Harvard University. He tried to persuade his wife to join him in law school. Ruth hesitated because she had some reservations about being a full-time student while taking care of one-year-old Jane.

Ginsburg later said that her father-in-law, Morris Ginsburg, helped convince her to enroll. He told her that no one would think any less of her if she decided not to go to law school. On the other hand, if she really wanted to be a lawyer, having a baby should not stand in her way. She said, "I realized that he was exactly right. If you want to do something badly enough, you find a way."[5]

3

Law School

With her excellent past academic record, Ruth Bader Ginsburg had no trouble getting into Harvard. Because she and her husband would both be attending classes, the Ginsburgs found a nanny for Jane. They arranged their schedules so that one of them would be at home when the sitter left at four o'clock every afternoon. Martin Ginsburg shared the household chores with his wife and took over almost all of the cooking duties. Early in their marriage, Ruth Bader Ginsburg demonstrated that cooking was not one of her talents. She prepared a tuna casserole that her husband called "as close to inedible as food could be."[1] Martin Ginsburg soon discovered that he liked to cook, and his wife relinquished her role in the kitchen.

As one of only nine women law students in a class of nearly five hundred men at Harvard University, Ginsburg experienced a number of episodes of gender discrimination. Early in her first year, the law school dean invited the nine women to a dinner at his home. He asked each one why she was taking a place in the class that could have been given to a man instead. Rather than challenge the rude and sexist remark, Ginsburg quietly replied that she wanted to learn about the law so she could understand her husband's work. She later said, "I did not think of myself as a feminist in the 1950s. The subject never even came up in my conversations with classmates or teachers."[2]

As the year progressed, Ruth Bader Ginsburg took her place at the top of the class. At the end of her freshman year, she was named to the staff of the *Harvard Law Review*, which was a periodical that contained legal editorials and articles. Only the top students were chosen to be on the *Law Review* staff. To be one of those selected was an honor, but the work required a great deal of extra time in the library and many additional hours of work at school.

During one of her *Law Review* work sessions, Ruth Ginsburg had to check a source in a certain section of the Harvard law school library. When she got there, she found that the particular room that she needed to use was closed to women. The off-limits room was a leftover symbol of the days when women were not permitted in the library at all. Ginsburg asked to have the periodical brought to the desk so that she could use it, but her request was denied. She returned to the *Law Review* office and had to send a male student to check the source for her.

Because there were so few women in law school during the 1950s, their performance was sometimes examined more closely than the work of their male counterparts. If a woman gave an incorrect answer in class, the mistake was more obvious because women were such a rarity in law school. Ginsburg's answers usually gave her professors and her fellow students little to criticize.

Many of her fellow students remember Ginsburg as an outstanding student. A former classmate, Ronald Loeb, later described Ginsburg during their law school days:

> While the rest of us were sulking around in dirty khaki pants and frayed button-down Oxford shirts, missing classes and complaining about all the work we had, you set a standard too high for any of us to achieve: you never missed classes; you were always prepared; your Law Review work was always done; you were always beautifully dressed and impeccably groomed; and you had a happy husband and a lovely young daughter.[3]

Ginsburg was also occasionally called Ruthless Ruthie by her classmates because of the intensity and dedication she exhibited at school.

It was not easy to juggle law school with motherhood, and Ginsburg confesses that she might have dropped out without the encouragement of her husband. She said, "What Martin did went far beyond support. He believed in me more than I believed in myself."[4] The couple took turns taking care of Jane so that each could attend class and spend the many hours in the library that are a necessary part of law school. After Jane went to bed and the house was quiet, Martin and Ruth Ginsburg often worked on their assignments late into the night.

Their careful scheduling and division of chores was blown apart during Ruth Bader Ginsburg's second year of law school. Her husband Martin was diagnosed with a usually fatal form of cancer of the lymph system. The lymph system, which is found throughout the body, produces white blood cells that help destroy the bacteria and viruses that enter the body.

The cancer that had invaded Martin Ginsburg's lymph system was very deadly. Doctors told the couple that chances for his recovery were almost zero. Two major surgeries were performed on Martin Ginsburg. In addition, massive doses of radiation were given to him in an attempt to destroy the cancer. During the months that he was undergoing radiation therapy, Martin Ginsburg was violently ill. He was not well enough to attend most of the classes in his final year of law school.

Instead of giving up and resigning herself to a bleak future, Ruth Ginsburg continued to attend her own classes and tried to go to most of her husband's classes as well. She took notes for him and typed the papers that he wrote so that he could keep up with his work at home. Ruth Bader Ginsburg later said, "We made a decision to take one day at a time. We never had a defeatist attitude. We were going to get through."[5] Thankfully, Martin Ginsburg survived, and his health slowly improved. The Ginsburgs would not know for another five years, though, whether Martin had been completely cured of the cancer he contracted.

When Martin Ginsburg graduated from law school, he was hired to work for a Manhattan law firm in New York City. Ruth still had another year of school left, so she transferred to Columbia University Law School for her final year. Once again, she made *Law Review*, and when she graduated in 1959, Ginsburg was tied for first place in the class. As Ruth Bader Ginsburg walked across the stage during the graduation ceremony, four-year-old Jane entertained the quiet gathering when she called out in a loud voice, "That's my Mommy."[6]

In spite of her high honors and impressive achievements, not a single law firm in New York City wanted to hire Ruth Bader Ginsburg after her graduation. It had only been during the past few years that Jews had been hired in the country's top law firms. They were simply not ready to hire women also. Ginsburg had three strikes against her since she was a woman, a Jew, and a mother.

Ginsburg's lack of employment opportunities was something of a surprise to her. She had worked for a

Ruth Bader and Martin Ginsburg (far right) pose with a group of friends in the 1950s.

large New York law firm during the summer between her second and third years of law school. Ruth Bader Ginsburg said, "I thought I had done a terrific job and I expected them to offer me a job on graduation."[7] They did not nor did anyone else. When she was asked years later if she was bitter about her lack of success in finding a job, she replied, "I don't think that being angry or being hostile is very productive." In order to bring about real change, "you have to do it through constant dialogue, constant persuasion, and not in shouting matches."[8]

Unable to find a job with a large law firm, Ginsburg applied for a clerk's job with Supreme Court Justice Felix Frankfurter. Justice Frankfurter asked an associate if Ginsburg wore skirts, because he could not stand girls in pants.[9] Even though he was assured that she wore appropriate clothing, Frankfurter never interviewed Ruth Bader Ginsburg for the clerk's job.

After a great deal of searching, Ginsburg was finally hired to clerk for United States District Judge Edmund Palmieri. That employment opportunity was only offered after Judge Palmieri was repeatedly assured by a law professor at Columbia that Ginsburg could handle both a career and motherhood. Ginsburg spent from 1959 until 1961 with Judge Palmieri. She said, "I worked probably harder than any other law clerk in the building, stayed late whenever it was necessary, sometimes when it wasn't necessary, came in Saturdays, and brought work home."[10]

The schedule around the Ginsburg house was a very busy one. Martin Ginsburg worked as a tax attorney, and he collected a large library of professional books at home. With the necessary reference materials at hand, he could do some of his work while he helped care for four-year-old Jane.

His wife also worked very long hours, both in the office and at home in the evening. Ruth Bader Ginsburg would not have been able to devote so much time to her work if it had not been for her husband's willingness to share child-rearing and household duties. Because of Martin Ginsburg's support, Ruth Bader Ginsburg was able to be an excellent clerk for Judge Palmieri and prove that she was very capable.

Twenty years after Ginsburg worked for him, Palmieri wrote that she was one of his "five best law clerks." He also said that Ginsburg "had fostered close and affectionate family ties and has been amply rewarded by a loving and charming family."[11] Her very successful clerkship with Judge Palmieri opened up a world of opportunities in the legal profession for Ruth Bader Ginsburg. Suddenly, top law firms were interested in hiring the very woman they had rejected two short years before. Ginsburg had her choice of jobs, but instead of going to work for a firm, she chose to return to the world of academia.

4

Columbia and Rutgers Universities

Ruth Bader Ginsburg accepted a position on the faculty of Columbia University Law School in 1961. She became a part of an international procedure project. Her part of the project involved a study of the Swedish judicial system. Ginsburg studied the Swedish language for several months and then made two trips to Sweden to do research. Her first trip lasted for four months, and six-year-old Jane joined her mother for several weeks during the summer. Martin Ginsburg also went to Sweden to be with his family for a short time during his vacation.

The next summer, mother and daughter traveled together to Sweden. Ginsburg's research led to the publication of a two-volume work called *Civil Procedure in Sweden*. It was coauthored with Anders Bruzelius and published in 1965. Jane remembers that she helped proofread the manuscript when she was just a little girl. She had been taught to read early by her mother and was quite a competent reader by the age of seven.

It was during her visits to Sweden that Ginsburg began to examine the different treatment that men and women received in the workplace. Swedish society was much more advanced than American society in granting equality to women. As Ginsburg compared the two cultures, she said that feminist feelings were stirred in her for the first time.[1]

By 1963, Ginsburg's part of the international project was completed, and she was offered an assistant professor's teaching position at Rutgers University Law School, located in Newark, New Jersey. She was only the second woman to join the faculty of the law school. In addition, Ginsburg was one of the first twenty women to teach in a law school anywhere in the United States.

Ruth Bader Ginsburg found that she liked being a teacher. She said, "There's a tremendous luxury in being a law teacher in that you can spend most of your time doing whatever interests you."[2] In addition to teaching classes, Ginsburg was free to study various areas of the law and then publish her findings.

In the classroom, Ruth Bader Ginsburg tried to present both sides of the issues that were under discussion, but she said, "I don't pretend to be neutral on issues when I am not. I like the students to understand that most of us have a perspective, most thinking people do. . . ."[3] As her skill in the classroom developed, Ginsburg faced a crisis of sorts in her personal life when she became pregnant with her second child.

Remembering her job demotion in Oklahoma when she was expecting Jane, Ruth Ginsburg decided not to report her current pregnancy to the university. She began to wear large, shapeless dresses to school in an attempt to camouflage her expanding waistline. The ploy worked, and son James was born at the end of the summer break, on September 8, 1965. Just weeks after the baby's birth, Ginsburg returned to her teaching duties for the fall term.

The following year was a difficult one for Ruth Bader Ginsburg. She now had an infant son to care for, along with ten-year-old Jane. Her critically ill father, Nathan Bader, had moved in with the family, and he also needed a great deal of special attention. Ginsburg had a long commute to school every day, from New York City to Newark, New Jersey. The time that she spent on the train each day at least gave her time to catch up on some of her reading and paperwork.

One day, during her early days at Rutgers, Ginsburg received a frantic phone call from her son's nanny. Two-year-old James had gotten into some cleaning supplies that were stored under the kitchen sink. He had picked up a bottle of an extremely caustic drain cleaning solution and drank some of the contents. Immediately the cleaner began to burn his mouth and throat. As soon as the nanny discovered what had happened, she wrapped the toddler in a blanket and rushed him to the hospital.

When Martin and Ruth Bader Ginsburg arrived at the hospital, they learned that their little son had very serious and potentially fatal burns to his face, mouth, and throat. After several long days and nights of uncertainty, the Ginsburgs were told by the doctor that their son would probably survive the accident.

James gradually recovered, but he was left with deep burns and severe scars on his face and mouth. During the following months, several reconstructive surgeries were performed in an effort to repair the damaged tissues. The surgery was successful, and the scars from the near-fatal accident were almost completely erased.

When Ginsburg recalled the horror of those weeks with James, she admitted to feelings of guilt that she was not there when the accident occurred. She also regretted that the drain cleaner was left within reach of the child.[4] She credits the child's nanny with doing exactly the right thing when she rushed the screaming toddler to the hospital. Any delay might have cost James his life.

Ruth Bader Ginsburg has always attempted to balance her professional life with her personal life, just as any working mother must do. While the children were growing up, both Ginsburg parents tried to be there when their son and daughter needed them. James later said:

> The family was always home for dinner. And a night did not go by when my mother did not check to see that I was doing my schoolwork. She was always there when I wanted her to be—and even when I didn't.[5]

James remembers that one morning he got up very early and found that his mother was still working at the dining room table. She had papers and books spread all over and had been eating a box of dried prunes, which was one of her favorite snacks. Ginsburg later said about her prodigious work habits: "I guess I work this way because I am so fussy about the quality of the product."[6] She often slept only three or four hours a night during the work week. On weekends, Ginsburg tried to catch up for all of the sleep that she missed during the week, and sometimes she slept for ten hours at a time.

Ginsburg's professional efforts were rewarded, and she moved from assistant to associate to full professor at Rutgers University during the 1960s. In 1969, the same year that she made full professor, she was also given tenure at Rutgers. Tenure, in the teaching profession, guarantees a professor's job for as long as that person wishes to remain on the staff of a particular school. The tenured employee cannot be dismissed unless a serious breach of contract takes place. It was a rare occurrence for women law professors to be offered tenure in the 1960s.

Martin, Ruth, James, and Jane Ginsburg enjoy a day on the water. The Ginsburg parents tried to be there when their son and daughter needed them.

It was during the late 1960s that women first began to be accepted in law schools in greater numbers than before. The United States' involvement in the Vietnam War continued to escalate, and more and more American men were being drafted into the armed forces. Therefore, there were fewer men available to apply to the nation's law schools. The schools began to turn to women applicants to help fill their classes.

In 1960, women made up only 2.5 percent of the total number of law students in the United States. By 1975 that number had risen to 15 percent, and by 1989, women made up over 40 percent of the classes in law schools across the country.[7]

During the late 1960s, when Ginsburg was a professor at Rutgers, the first gender discrimination complaints started to be filed in U.S. courts. Ginsburg had not really investigated the subject of women's rights before. To better acquaint herself with the topic, she spent several weeks in the law library. She read articles and previous cases that concerned the unequal treatment of men and women. She found that there were very few instances in the literature that supported a woman's right to equality. At the end of her research, she wondered, "How have people been putting up with such arbitrary distinctions? How have I been putting up with them?"[8]

5

The Fight for Women's Rights

Ruth Bader Ginsburg was a prime example of the second-class status that was commonly assigned to women. She clearly had talent far beyond that of many male law students, but she was denied employment after graduation because of her gender. Ginsburg's dilemma was not unique. A male-dominated society had been in place throughout most of the history of the United States.

In America's past, men made the laws, ran the government, and conducted all of the nation's important business. Most women were delegated the tasks of raising children and keeping house. Although child-rearing is a very important job, it is far from the only thing that women are capable of doing. Unfortunately, women who wished to step outside of their assigned roles often found the doors closed to them.

Most American women accepted their fate and performed their expected duties. There were some, however, who chose to fight the system and seek more equal treatment for themselves and their sisters. The first organized push for women's rights occurred in Seneca Falls, New York, in 1848. Two of the organizers, Elizabeth Cady Stanton and Lucretia Mott, called on the three hundred assembled participants to demand equal rights for women in areas such as employment, political life, education, and voting privileges, or suffrage.

During the next few decades, women made very few advances in any of those areas. In 1870, the recently ratified Fifteenth Amendment to the Constitution prohibited states from discriminating against voters because of race or former status as slaves. It gave African-American men the right to vote but excluded all women. The demand for suffrage for all Americans continued to be a rallying cry for feminist groups.

In 1875 Virginia Minor brought a civil suit before the U.S. Supreme Court. In it, she tried to defend her right to vote in national elections and based her suit on a provision of the Fourteenth Amendment to the Constitution. The provision said: "No state shall make or enforce any law which shall abridge the privileges or immunities of citizens of the United States."[1] The Supreme Court rejected her argument and stated that "the Fourteenth Amendment did not confer the right to vote on women any more than it conferred such a right on children, the insane, or criminals."[2] The fight for women's suffrage continued unsuccessfully, in spite of the work of many dedicated advocates.

A new century began, and still women could not vote in most states or hold public office. In 1913 President Woodrow Wilson rejected a plea to amend the Constitution to give suffrage to women. He said that the states, not the federal government, should control the right to vote. Then, in 1917, America entered World War I. During the next several months, over one million women went to work in the United States to replace the men who were called to serve in the armed forces. Women worked in munitions factories, assembled tanks, and helped keep the country running.

It soon became apparent to President Wilson that women were just as dedicated and competent as their male counterparts. In 1918 Wilson went before the United States Senate to urge the members to approve an amendment that would allow women to vote. He said that American women had become partners in the war for democratic freedom, "but shall we admit them only to a partnership of suffering and not to a partnership of privilege and right?"[3]

One year later the Nineteenth Amendment was passed with a two-thirds majority in the House of Representatives and Senate and was sent to the states for ratification. On August 26, 1920, after being ratified by three-quarters of the states, the Nineteenth Amendment to the Constitution became law. All American women were finally guaranteed the right to vote.

Ruth Bader Ginsburg said about the 1920 decision finally to permit women's suffrage:

> Times change, and eventually, after nearly a century of struggle, women achieved the vote, and they became full citizens, and many people thought that when women became full citizens entitled to the vote, they had achieved equality that made them full and equal citizens with men, entitled to the same equal protection before the laws.[4]

Unfortunately, the right to vote did not automatically erase the other inequalities that women faced in their daily lives. Many still held low-paying jobs and were restricted to positions as secretaries, nurses, clerks, and teachers. Very few women were doctors, lawyers, or business executives. In 1930 there were only an estimated 150 female dentists in the entire United States.[5] Even when women did the same work as men, they were usually paid less.

In order to try to eliminate wage discrimination in the workplace, President John Kennedy signed the Equal Pay Act, which went into effect in 1964. It required that the same pay be given to women when they did the same jobs as men. Many companies got around the new ruling by changing job descriptions so that men's work and women's work were defined in different terms.

As more and more women entered the workforce, they were faced with the prospect of a lifetime of low wages. By 1960, 37.7 percent of women were in the labor force in the United States.[6] Some were looking for a second income so that their families could afford to buy more "extras." Other women were simply trying to make enough money to keep food on the table for their children.

As large numbers of women entered the job market, the occasions for gender discrimination rose steadily. In most instances, female employees simply accepted their secondary status and did not complain about poor treatment or low wages. There were those, though, who chose to fight for their rights. They filed complaints and grievances with the courts and with the American Civil Liberties Union (ACLU). The ACLU was founded in 1920 to help protect and defend the constitutional rights of all Americans. The organization provided free counseling and legal representation to clients who thought that their civil liberties were in jeopardy.

About the time that the first gender discrimination cases were being filed, Ruth Bader Ginsburg was a professor at Rutgers University Law School. In addition to her teaching duties, Ginsburg also did some work with the New Jersey branch of the American Civil Liberties Union. Because she was a woman, the gender discrimination cases that were filed with the ACLU were often referred to her.

Ginsburg later said:

Both the ACLU and my students prodded me to take an active part in the effort to eliminate senseless gender lines in the law. Once I became involved, I found the legal work fascinating and had high hopes for significant change in the next decade.[7]

Indeed there was significant change in the issue of women's equality during the next ten years. A great deal of it would come about because of the efforts of Ruth Bader Ginsburg.

In 1970, partly because of the increased numbers of women in the nation's law schools, a new awareness about women's issues began to surface. The media took up the topic, and a number of articles appeared that addressed the equal rights movement. By 1970 more than 10 percent of law students were women. Courses concerning women's rights started to appear on class schedules. Also, new textbooks were written that contained fewer sexist statements than those that were used in the past.

Early in the 1970s, there was also a push to get an amendment to the Constitution passed that would guarantee women's rights. The Equal Rights Amendment (ERA) was first proposed to Congress in 1923, but no progress was made on its passage until nearly fifty years later. By the 1970s, the amendment read: "Equality of rights under the law shall not be denied or abridged by the United States or any State on account of sex."[8]

In 1971 the ERA was approved by a two-thirds vote in the United States House of Representatives. In 1972 it was also approved by a two-thirds vote in the United States Senate. The final hurdle in the amendment's passage was its ratification by three-quarters of the states by the June 30, 1982, deadline. As the date approached, a last ditch effort to insure passage was made in several key states. In Illinois, some ERA proponents chained themselves together at the door of the state senate chamber in an attempt to draw attention to their cause. Other backers staged a hunger strike to emphasize their dedication to gender equality.

In spite of the efforts of many women, only thirty-five states had voted to ratify the Equal Rights Amendment by the 1982 deadline. In order for the ERA to become law, approval was needed by thirty-eight states. Fifty-nine years after it was first proposed, the amendment failed to become a part of the Constitution of the United States.

During those years, many women were involved in the attempt to gain passage of the ERA. Ginsburg echoed her support for the amendment when she wrote:

> We believe in racial equality, we believe in free speech. We have recorded those beliefs in the Constitution, our fundamental instrument of government. We are advancing toward the belief that men and women should be seen as equal before the law. We should record that basic principle in the Constitution.[9]

Ratification of the ERA was just one approach in the efforts being made for gender equality. Another avenue for change would take place in the courtroom. Ruth Bader Ginsburg became involved in that legal maneuvering when she wrote a brief for, but did not argue, the case of *Reed* v. *Reed*, a landmark women's rights case.

Women's Rights
and the ACLU

The history making case of *Reed* v. *Reed* was brought before the Supreme Court by attorneys who represented Mrs. Sally Reed of Boise, Idaho. Mrs. Reed had been denied permission by the lower courts to be the executor of her deceased son's estate. Instead, Mrs. Reed's former husband was made the executor of the estate, because an Idaho law preferred men over women in such cases.

After all the arguments were heard before the nine Supreme Court Justices, Chief Justice Warren Burger wrote the opinion for the case. As the Court's representative, he said that gender discrimination was evident in *Reed* v. *Reed*, and presented "the very kind of arbitrary legislative choice forbidden by the Equal Protection Clause" of the Fourteenth Amendment to the U.S. Constitution.[1] It was the first time that the

Supreme Court had declared a law unconstitutional because it discriminated on the basis of gender. After the historic decision, Mrs. Reed said:

> We never dreamed it would go this far. I just cared about the principle of the thing. The courts don't give women the right to be heard. I hope more women will do what I did. Instead of complaining about the way things are, we've got to go into the courts and get them changed.[2]

Shortly after the *Reed* v. *Reed* decision, Ruth Bader Ginsburg was offered a full professorship at Columbia University Law School. She accepted the position and taught constitutional law there from 1972 until 1980. In addition to her classes, she was also involved on a part-time basis with the ACLU. Since women's rights had taken a place in the forefront of the fight for equality, the ACLU board of directors voted in 1972 to establish the Women's Rights Project (WRP). Ginsburg was the project's founder, and she served as its general counsel from 1973 to 1980.

It was during Ginsburg's tenure on the WRP that the laws of the land in regard to women's rights were gradually changed. The entire process of equality for the sexes had to be approached very carefully. Women were traditionally viewed as homemakers and mothers, and men were seen as providers. Ginsburg later said about the stereotypes, "When I graduated from law school in 1959, it was not possible to move legislators or judges

Ruth Bader Ginsburg was a professor at Columbia University Law School from 1972 to 1980.

toward recognition of a sex-equality principle. The idea was unfamiliar and therefore unacceptable."[3]

Ginsburg and her associates on the WRP had to select their cases very carefully. She said that their strategy:

> . . . was to bring a series of cases, each maximally suited to a favorable court response, each serving as a foundation for its immediate successor and each taking the reasoning one step closer to constitutionally guaranteed sexual equality.[4]

Ginsburg added:

> My hope . . . was that the judges might look and realize that this is a very large and important matter; so that we would guard against the tendency some might have who don't know and haven't thought about it, to see these cases almost as a joke.[5]

With those goals in mind, the WRP began to examine the cases that might serve as stepping stones in their efforts to guarantee the rights of American women. Ginsburg also spent much of her time publicizing the second-class status of women as she spoke to her classes and to various organizations. In addition, she published many papers and articles in order to help build up a body of literature on the subject of gender inequality. In 1974, along with Kenneth Davidson and Herma Hill Kay, Ginsburg wrote a book called *Text, Cases, and Materials on Sex-Based Discrimination.* All of Ginsburg's writings helped establish a collection of legal opinions concerning women's rights.

Frontiero v. *Richardson* (1973) was the name of the first case that Ruth Bader Ginsburg argued before the Supreme Court. The case revealed that Lieutenant Sharon Frontiero, an Air Force physical therapist, was unable to obtain health and housing benefits for her husband. Military men automatically received such benefits for their wives and families. A woman in the military had to prove that she provided more than half of her husband's support before her family could collect the same benefits. The difference in benefits was based entirely on the gender of the service person. Ginsburg said:

> We wanted to get rid of these gender labels in the law. *Frontiero* was a very good case to do that because it could easily be perceived as a straight equal pay case. Two people in the military, both the same rank, one gets more than the other.[6]

On May 14, 1973, the U.S. Supreme Court ruled that all military personnel of comparable rank must receive the same benefits, regardless of gender. Justice William Brennan, Jr., wrote in the majority opinion:

> There can be no doubt that our nation has had a long and unfortunate history of sex discrimination. Traditionally, such discrimination was rationalized by an attitude of 'romantic paternalism' which, in practical effect, put women not on a pedestal but in a cage.[7]

After the Supreme Court decision in the *Frontiero* case, Ginsburg said:

> It is the most far-reaching and important ruling on sex discrimination to come out of the Supreme Court yet. It will spell the beginning of reforms in hundreds of statutes which do not give equal benefits to men and women.[8]

In 1972, women made up more than 40 percent of the workforce of the United States, but they were usually paid only about half as much in salary as men. The positive outcome of the *Frontiero* case was a beginning, but many more decisions would have to be made in favor of women before anything approaching equality in the workplace was reached.

With a major Supreme Court victory behind her, Ginsburg described her feelings as she appeared before the Justices for the first time. She said:

> I was terribly nervous. In fact, I didn't eat lunch for fear that I might throw up. Two minutes into my argument, the fear dissolved. Suddenly, I realized that here before me were the nine leading jurists of America, a captive audience. I felt a surge of power that carried me through.[9]

Ruth Bader Ginsburg was not as successful with her second Supreme Court case, *Kahn* v. *Shevin* (1974). She represented a man who challenged a Florida law that allowed women a small tax exemption after their husbands died. The state viewed the women as economically disadvantaged when they became widows. After hearing the testimony in the case, the nine Justices upheld the law as it was written and allowed the tax break to continue for women.

Ginsburg's third case, *Weinberger* v. *Wisenfeld*, concerned a husband's inability to collect benefits. Paula Wisenfeld, a New Jersey schoolteacher and the family's primary wage earner, died while giving birth to a son. Stephen Wisenfeld attempted to collect his wife's Social Security benefits. He wanted to be able to remain at home and take care of his child until the boy entered first grade. He was denied access to the benefits because the Social Security Act of 1930 only listed women as dependents.

Ginsburg's arguments in the *Wisenfeld* case revolved around the stereotype that women are homemakers while men are providers. In presenting her arguments before the Court, she attempted "to show that the real issue was not a narrow women's rights question, but a question about people's freedom to organize their lives on the basis of their own judgment."[10] The Supreme Court Justices listened to Ginsburg's arguments and again ruled in her favor. Paula Wisenfeld had paid the same Social Security taxes as a man and was entitled to the same protection for her family.

Ginsburg's tactics in selecting her cases was very shrewd. Since gender discrimination was a relatively new topic in the courts, she carefully approached the subject from an interesting angle. She did not jump right into the issue of the unequal treatment of women under the law. Instead, she selected cases that demonstrated that men were sometimes victims because of gender classification rules. "Her plan, like Marshall's strategy in attacking segregation 40 years earlier, was to gradually lead the Supreme Court to strike down laws that arbitrarily treated men and women differently."[11]

Kathleen Peratis, former staff director of the WRP said that Ginsburg:

> . . . had a real vision of where she wanted to go and what she had to do to get there. . . . She is my idol. I named my daughter after her. I told my daughter that her namesake would be the first woman to sit on the Supreme Court. It turns out I was only off by one.[12]

Ruth Bader Ginsburg was certainly getting a lot of firsthand experience. Under her direction, the Women's Rights Project of the ACLU continued to win case after case in the Supreme Court. In *Craig* v. *Boren* (1976), the Supreme Court overturned a law in Oklahoma that said that men had to be twenty-one-years-old to buy beer but women could buy beer at age eighteen. Lawmakers argued that more men would drive after they had been drinking and so they should be denied access to alcohol until they were older. The Supreme Court ruled that the law discriminated on the basis of gender and was therefore unconstitutional.

In *Califano* v. *Goldfarb* (1977), Mr. Goldfarb applied to collect his deceased wife's Social Security benefits, and his request was denied. When the Court heard the arguments in the case, they ruled in favor of Mr. Goldfarb. His wife had fulfilled all of the requirements for Social Security protection. The same rules that applied to men should also apply to women. Therefore, Mr. Goldfarb was eligible to receive the benefits, just as Mr. Wisenfeld had been.

Duren v. *Missouri* (1979) was Ginsburg's final Supreme Court victory during the 1970s. A Missouri law allowed women to be excused from jury duty if they did not wish to serve. They simply had to make a request, and they were exempted. Once again, the Supreme Court observed that men and women were held to different standards and struck down the law.

Case by case, Ruth Bader Ginsburg helped change the laws that treated men and women unequally. Kathleen Peratis said about her coworker on the WRP, "Her work was very clear, very orderly. She never guessed, she never weaseled, she was always thoroughly prepared. She always knew all the facts and all the law of every case she cited."[13] That attention to detail meant very long work days for Ruth Bader Ginsburg, days that often exceeded twelve hours.

It was during some of those days at work that Ginsburg received a number of phone calls from the principal at the school that her son James attended. The rambunctious boy was often a little more than his teachers could handle. The calls increased in frequency until Ruth Bader Ginsburg finally told the principal that

James had two parents. She requested that the calls of complaint be equally directed to Mr. Ginsburg. After that the calls decreased.

Ruth Bader Ginsburg continued to fight for women's rights in the courts and in her personal life as well. She succeeded in winning five of the six cases that she argued before the Supreme Court in the 1970s. She laid the foundation for gender equality under the law and is often called the Thurgood Marshall of the women's movement. It was her successes before the Court, and her stellar reputation among her associates, that led to Ginsburg's next assignment.

7

Judge Ginsburg

In 1980, President Jimmy Carter nominated Ruth Bader Ginsburg to be a judge for the United States Court of Appeals for the District of Columbia circuit. She would be one of about 175 judges who serve on the thirteen circuit courts that are located throughout the United States. The appeals courts hear cases that have already been tried in other federal courts. When a person receives an unfavorable ruling in a lower court, that person has the right to appeal the decision to a higher court. The courts that Ginsburg would be a part of are the last step in the judicial process before a case goes on to the Supreme Court.

The cases that came before the United States circuit courts were usually concerned with possible mistakes that had been made in the way a previous trial was conducted or a judicial ruling made. The attorneys involved in the appeal had to file details of the case, or briefs, with the court of appeals. The attorneys were sometimes then allowed to present their arguments before a panel of three judges.

After the oral arguments in the case were heard, the three judges took time to privately study the case before they issued a written opinion. Ginsburg, upon her confirmation by the United States Senate, became one of the judges who heard appeal cases for the circuit court that was located in the Washington, D.C., area.

The number of cases that are appealed has increased steadily during the past decades. Many litigants file appeal after appeal in an attempt to have a judgment overturned in a higher court. That is especially true in death penalty cases. Some are appealed right up to the time that an execution is carried out. The courts of appeals are just one step in the lengthy process, and their judges have a steady number of cases on which to rule. Their workload is often formidable, but Ginsburg was accustomed to a busy schedule.

By 1980, when she was appointed to the bench, Ruth and Martin Ginsburg's children had grown older. Daughter Jane Ginsburg was a twenty-five-year-old graduate of the University of Chicago, where she earned both bachelor's and master's degrees. She was also a recent graduate of Harvard Law School. James was fifteen years old and a high school student.

The Ginsburgs moved to Washington, D.C., so Ruth Bader Ginsburg could take her place on the court of appeals. Martin Ginsburg left behind in New York City a successful law practice as a mergers and acquisitions specialist. He became a professor at Georgetown University Law School. In addition to his teaching duties, Martin Ginsburg also occasionally represented a few interesting cases in court.

Soon after Ginsburg became a judge, a historical event took place in the United States. In 1981, President Ronald Reagan appointed Sandra Day O'Connor to be the first female Supreme Court Justice. Fifty-one-year-old O'Connor was a graduate of Stanford University Law School, a former Arizona state senator, and a judge. In the Supreme Court's history, 101 men had served as Justices, but no woman had ever before been appointed to that lofty position.

Ruth Bader Ginsburg wrote about the appointment of O'Connor:

> The brightest signal of the changed complexion of our profession is the appointment of Sandra Day O'Connor to the Supreme Court. Even on that highest court, I predict that within the decade women's place will no longer be singular.[1]

Ginsburg was off by only two years. Her own appointment to the Supreme Court did not take place until twelve years after the appointment of O'Connor.

Ginsburg settled into her new job on the court of appeals with her usual dedication to detail. One of her

In 1980, Ruth Bader Ginsburg was appointed to be a judge for the United States Court of Appeals.

former clerks later said that Ginsburg "was always, always, always thoroughly prepared."[2] She sometimes put the lawyers who stood before her on the spot as she closely questioned their cases. She did her homework and expected others to do the same. David Post, who clerked for Ginsburg during her tenure on the court of appeals, said that he often got work back from her that had been "totally torn apart. Every word examined, literally. It was very painful. But I'll be forever in her debt, because that's what the law is—language."[3]

When Ginsburg was on the bench, she appeared to be very serious and carefully weighed the words that she used. Occasionally she became impatient with the attorneys before her, but as one former clerk said, "I never knew her to lose her temper. She could be intense, but never angry."[4] Away from the courtroom, Ginsburg often showed a personal interest in the people who worked with her.

She kept in touch with the various clerks in her office and scheduled a reunion every year for them and their families. She performed a wedding ceremony for one of her clerks. When she sent a gift to the newborn son of another clerk, she also included a present for the baby's four-year-old-sister so the older child would not feel left out. Many of her best clerks in the court of appeals went on to the Supreme Court to work for one of the nine Justices. Their training, at the hands of Ginsburg, prepared them very well for their duties in the highest court.

In a case that Ruth Bader Ginsburg heard on the court of appeals, one of the attorneys involved requested a continuance, or postponement, of the case. His wife was going to have a baby, and he wanted to stay at home for a time to help care for the child. When the other two judges on the bench said no to the request, Ginsburg asked for a private conference with her associates. In a later statement, she reported:

> I said, 'Here is a man telling us that he is going to take care of the baby' and all the votes turned around. [Suddenly there was some] consciousness that the job—taking care of children—can and should be a man's job. And when a man says he's doing it, his work as a parent should be respected fully.[5]

In Ruth Bader Ginsburg's own life, her husband Martin Ginsburg had played such a prominent role in the sharing of duties that are so often assigned only to women. He was certainly an equal partner in the couple's household and child-rearing tasks. Without his help, Ginsburg might never have attained the position that she held on the court of appeals. Her wish was for all women to have the opportunities that she had experienced. She expressed those wishes in a 1986 article titled "Special versus Equal Treatment" when she wrote:

> . . . were I Queen, my principle affirmative action plan would have three legs. First, it would promote equal educational opportunity and effective job training for women, so that they would not be

reduced to dependency on a man or on the state. Second, my plan would give men encouragement and incentives to share more evenly with women the joys, responsibilities, worries, upsets and sometimes tedium of raising children from infancy to adulthood. Third, the plan would make quality day care available from infancy on. Children in my ideal world would not be women's priorities, they would be human priorities.[6]

Ruth Bader Ginsburg served for thirteen years on the circuit court of appeals. She listened to hundreds of cases and wrote opinions for more than three hundred of those cases. She was praised as being a cautious, moderate judge. Ginsburg told Deborah Merritt, her former law clerk, that she liked being a judge and that ". . . she had found her place and that she liked dealing with the grand issues in individual cases."[7] Ginsburg would soon have the opportunity to deal with even larger issues, perhaps some of the most important issues in the nation.

8

Supreme Court Nomination

When Supreme Court Justice Byron White announced his plans for retirement, it became President Bill Clinton's responsibility to select a replacement for him. Since the nine Justices on the Supreme Court serve for life, a vacancy does not occur very often. Clinton carefully considered more than forty candidates in his search for a new Justice.

One of the possibilities that President Clinton considered very carefully was Ruth Bader Ginsburg. After Clinton learned more about Ginsburg from his advisors, he invited her to the White House for a ninety-minute interview on June 13, 1993. After the interview, Ginsburg went home and waited to hear the outcome of her visit with the President. Late that same night, Clinton called Ginsburg and offered the Supreme

Court appointment to her. Following her acceptance, a whirlwind of activity descended on the formerly private lives of Ruth Bader and Martin Ginsburg.

On June 14, 1993, the day after the conversation with President Clinton, Ginsburg was suddenly thrust into the spotlight. Reporters dug into her background so they could write stories for their newspapers. Television crews waited to interview the Supreme Court nominee, and soon she could be seen on television screens across the United States and the world. Ruth Bader Ginsburg was no longer just another face in the crowd, and her activities were carefully followed during the weeks and months ahead.

Before she could take her place among the other Supreme Court Justices, Ginsburg had to attend confirmation hearings. An eighteen-member Senate Judiciary Committee was scheduled to question Ginsburg about her life and views. If the committee decided that the President's choice was acceptable, they would then pass her name on for a full Senate vote. During the next few weeks, Ginsburg would have to carefully prepare for the hearings. Her confirmation depended in large part on what she said before the Judiciary Committee members.

As Ginsburg poured over her writings and legal opinions of the past thirty-four years, friends and family members called to offer their congratulations and support. Dozens of flower arrangements arrived at Ginsburg's home and office. Because she received so many flowers, she kept the congratulatory cards and letters and sent many of the flowers on to the area hospitals for the patients to enjoy. In order to better familiarize herself with the confirmation process, Ginsburg also watched video tapes of some recent hearings.

Members of the Senate Judiciary Committee were also busy reviewing the history of Ruth Bader Ginsburg's legal philosophy. She had published many papers during her tenure as a professor at Rutgers and Columbia law schools. Her historic work with the ACLU in the 1970s was scrutinized, as were the more than three hundred opinions that Ginsburg wrote during her years as a judge. The committee had a great deal of information to process and consider as they prepared to question the Supreme Court nominee.

On July 20, 1993, Ginsburg took her place at a table in front of the eighteen members of the Senate Judiciary committee, headed by Democratic Senator Joseph Biden of Delaware. Seated behind Ginsburg were members of her family, friends, the press, and other interested spectators. Television cameras and microphones would record every word that was spoken during the three-day hearing.

Ginsburg began her remarks by saying:

> The president's confidence in my capacity to serve as a Supreme Court Justice is responsible for the proceedings about to begin. There are no words to tell him what is in my heart. I can say simply this. If confirmed, I will try in every way to justify his faith in me."[1]

Ginsburg went on to say:

> Supreme Court Justices are guardians of the great
> charter that has served as our nation's fundamental
> instrument of government for over 200 years. It is
> the oldest written Constitution still in force in the
> world. . . . Serving on this court is the highest
> honor, the most awesome trust that can be placed
> in a judge. It means working at my craft, working
> with and for the law as a way to keep our society
> both ordered and free.[2]

In order to approve Ginsburg's nomination, the
senators needed to know more about the candidate's
views on a number of issues. When Ruth Bader
Ginsburg was asked about her opinion concerning a
women's right to abortion, she answered:

> This is something central to a woman's life, to her
> dignity. It's a decision that she must make for
> herself. And when government controls that
> decision for her, she's being treated as less than a
> fully adult human responsible for her own
> choices.[3]

Ginsburg's personal views were less evident when she
was asked by Utah Republican Senator Orrin Hatch to
address the issue of the death penalty in capital crimes.
Ginsburg answered repeatedly that death penalty cases
were an issue that she would probably have to rule on if
she were confirmed to a seat on the Supreme Court.
Therefore, she could not make any comments about the
issue during the confirmation process.[4] Pennsylvania

Republican Senator Arlen Specter then attempted to get Ginsburg to state her opinion concerning the death penalty, but she resisted his efforts also.

The discussion then moved on to the topic of the Fourteenth Amendment to the Constitution, the amendment that granted equal protection to all United States citizens. In her comments to Senator Specter, Ginsburg said, "It's a sad part of our history, Sen. Specter, but it is part of our history that at the time of the 14th Amendment, that great amendment that changed so much in this nation, it didn't change the status of women."[5]

It was not until passage of the Nineteenth Amendment in 1920 that women were finally given the right to vote. And it was not until the 1970s, when Ruth Bader Ginsburg successfully argued five gender discrimination cases before the Supreme Court, that women began to experience less gender bias. The positive outcome of those five cases was a small step toward the equal treatment of women.

Ruth Bader Ginsburg still supported the idea of an equal rights amendment to the Constitution. In her confirmation hearings, she expressed those beliefs when she said:

> I remain an advocate of the Equal Rights Amendment, I will tell you, for this reason: because I have a daughter and a granddaughter, and I would like the legislature of this country and of all the states to stand up and say we know what that history was in the 19th century and we want to make a clarion call that women and men are equal before the law . . . .[6]

As the second woman on the Supreme Court, Ginsburg would bring her experience as a women's rights advocate to the bench with her. She had suffered discrimination at the hands of the system but later successfully fought to eliminate some of that gender bias. Ginsburg had also been a victim of another kind of discrimination that was a result of her Jewish heritage. During her childhood, Ginsburg remembered riding in the car with her parents and seeing a sign in a store window that read: "No Dogs or Jews Allowed."[7]

Instead of making her bitter and resentful, Ruth Bader Ginsburg's past experiences appeared to make her an advocate for tolerance. During her confirmation hearings, Ginsburg related an experience that had happened to her many years before. After a several-month stay in Sweden, Ginsburg returned to New York City. In Sweden, a large number of that country's people have blonde hair, blue eyes, and fair skin. While she rode on the New York subway, Ginsburg noticed that the people around her had such a variety of skin colors and appearances, unlike the Swedish people.

According to Ginsburg, she looked at those who were seated around her and then thought:

> What a wonderful country we live in—people who are so different in so many ways, and yet we, for the most part, get along with each other. The richness of the diversity of this country is a treasure, and it's a constant challenge, too, to remain tolerant and respectful of one another.[8]

During the confirmation proceedings, when Ginsburg was asked by Wisconsin Democratic Senator Herb Kohl how she wanted people to think of her, she answered, "As someone who cares about people and does the best she can with the talent she has to make a contribution to a better world."[9]

After three days of public testimony, a session of private questioning was scheduled to be held with just the members of the Judiciary Committee and Ginsburg. It would allow the senators an opportunity to talk about any issues in the nominee's background or career where they had insufficient information. A transcript of the session would be available to any United States senator who wanted to see it, but it would otherwise be confidential.

After all of the questions had been answered and all of the important issues discussed, the Senate Judiciary Committee voted 18–0 in favor of Judge Ginsburg. The eighteen members of the committee then passed her name on for a full Senate vote. By a vote of 96 to 3, the United States Senate confirmed the nomination of Ruth Bader Ginsburg on August 3, 1993. Democratic Senator Donald Riegle of Michigan was absent and did not vote. By almost unanimous agreement, Ruth Bader Ginsburg was named to be the 107th Justice of the United States Supreme Court.

In only two months, the Supreme Court would begin its fall term. There was a great deal for Justice

Ginsburg to do to prepare for her new appointment. Retiring Justice Byron White had been saving various materials for his replacement to review. Also, in the month of September, the Court decided which new cases to hear during the following term. Because her confirmation had been completed so quickly, Justice Ginsburg was able to participate in that selection process. But, before the fall term began, Ruth Bader Ginsburg needed some time to move into her office and settle into her new role as the 107th Supreme Court Justice.

9

History of the Supreme Court

The role that Justice Ruth Ginsburg was about to fill was established more than two hundred years before, during the formation of the United States government. On May 25, 1787, fifty-five delegates met in the State House in Philadelphia, Pennsylvania. Among them were George Washington, Ben Franklin, and James Madison. During the next four months, the men would gather nearly every day to argue and debate about how the United States should be governed. Finally, after many long and difficult sessions, they presented a four-page document to the country that was known as the United States Constitution.

Power in the new government was divided among three separate areas. The executive branch would be headed by a President, who was elected by the people.

Ruth Bader Ginsburg is sworn in as an Associate Justice of the Supreme Court, as President Bill Clinton looks on.

The legislative branch would consist of the United States Senate and House of Representatives and would be charged with making the laws. The judicial branch would enforce the laws, and its highest office would be the Supreme Court.

The three branches were designed to work together, but each part of the new government was independent of the other two. The framers of the Constitution established three separate governing bodies to insure that a system of checks and balances was in place and that no one branch could gain total control of the United States government.

The Constitution called for a federal judiciary, but exact details of the United States legal system had to be developed. The first bill that was introduced by the new United States Senate was the Judiciary Act of 1789. It created thirteen federal district courts. They were the first level in the federal legal system, followed by the circuit courts on the middle level. The Supreme Court would be the highest Court in the land and would be located in the nation's capital.

New York City was the capital of the United States when the Supreme Court first met in the Royal Exchange Building on February 1, 1790. The original Court consisted of John Jay, who was appointed by President George Washington to be the first Chief Justice, and five Associate Justices. All six of the members of the first Supreme Court were attorneys who had been involved in the creation of the United States Constitution.

In February, 1790, the Supreme Court convened for the first time in the Royal Exchange Building in New York City.

The Supreme Court met in New York City for only one year. The capital of the nation was moved to Philadelphia, Pennsylvania, in 1790. In Philadelphia, the Supreme Court first had chambers in Independence Hall and then in city hall. During the next few years, a site on the Potomac River at the Virginia and Maryland border was selected for the nation's permanent capital. After the swamp and farm land was cleared, construction of the White House began in 1792, followed by initial work on the U.S. Capitol in 1793.

In 1800 the Supreme Court moved to Washington, in the District of Columbia, and first held court in an unfinished basement room in the United States Capitol. In the ensuing years, the Supreme Court moved from chamber to chamber until Congress authorized the construction of a Supreme Court Building in 1929. The cornerstone for the building was laid on October 13, 1932, and the construction was completed in 1934 at a cost of nearly $10 million.

The United States Supreme Court building is built of marble. The main corridor is known as the Great Hall, and at its end, doors open into the Supreme Court chamber. The chamber itself is not large. It contains rows of benches that seat only about two hundred people. Directly in front of the Justices are rows of chairs for the many lawyers that are connected with each case that is being heard.

Also on the main floor are the Justices' chambers and additional offices for staff members. The building's

During the late 1700s, the Supreme Court met in the Philadelphia, Pennsylvania City Hall.

second floor contains more offices, a library reading room, and the Justice's dining room. On the third floor is a 300,000 volume library. Under the main floor, at ground level, are rooms occupied by the clerk of the Court and the curator, in addition to offices for business and the press. The Court currently employs more than three hundred people and its budget exceeds $20 million a year.[1]

By the time the Supreme Court was finally able to move into its own home in 1935, there were nine Justices on the bench. The number had changed over the years, from six to seven to nine, and had remained at nine since 1869. In the Court's history, there have been only sixteen Chief Justices and ninety-five Associate Justices, for a total of 106 individual members. Ruth Bader Ginsburg would be the 107th Justice to serve on the United States Supreme Court. It was a historic institution that still retained in the 1990s much of the tradition of the first Court.

White quill pens have traditionally been placed on the counsel tables every day that the Court is in session. They appear today just as they did in the days of the early Court. Also, the traditional seal of the Supreme Court is used to stamp official papers. Today's seal, which is similar to the Great Seal of the United States, is only the fifth one in use in the history of the Court.

The Supreme Court is in session each year from the first Monday in October until late June or early July.

The Supreme Court met for many years in the United States
Capitol building in Washington, D.C.

The 10:00 A.M. arrival of the Justices in the courtroom is announced by the marshal. All of those who are present in the chamber rise and remain standing while he gives the traditional chant:

> The Honorable, the Chief Justice and the Associate Justices of the Supreme Court of the United States. Oyez (hear ye)! Oyez! Oyez! All persons having business before the Honorable, the Supreme Court of the United States, are admonished to draw near and give their attention, for the Court is now sitting. God save the United States and this Honorable Court![2]

After the chant, the Justices sit down, followed by those in attendance.

Usually the Court hears cases for a period of two weeks and then spends two weeks in private study and conference in order to review the cases and write opinions. The number of cases that the Supreme Court considers for a hearing has risen steadily over the years. In 1960, 2,296 cases were on the docket, but that number rose to 5,144 in 1980. Currently the Court must study more than 7,000 petitions each year and decide which ones will be heard. During the past several years, the Court has written opinions for 107 to 130 of those cases.[3]

There have been many Supreme Court decisions that have changed the way that Americans live their daily lives. In the beginning, the Court was charged with ". . . ensuring the American people the promise of

In 1934, construction was completed on the Supreme Court building in Washington, D.C.

equal Justice under the law, and, thereby, also functions as guardian and interpreter of the Constitution."[4] The Constitution was intentionally written in rather general terms so that future generations could interpret its meaning in relation to changing social conditions.

Ruth Bader Ginsburg would have as her task the job of relating the original intent of the Constitution to cases in the 1990s. More than two hundred years had passed since the original document was written, and interpretation could become very involved when today's standards were applied. There were no easy decisions to be made, and each case that was heard required a great deal of preparation and thought. Ruth Bader Ginsburg's background as an equal rights advocate and a judge had hopefully prepared her for the monumental task that lay in her future.

10

Past and Present

Justice Ruth Bader Ginsburg selected for her Supreme Court office the rooms that had been occupied by the late Justice Thurgood Marshall. The chambers were located on the second floor of the Supreme Court building. The other eight Justices had their offices on the first floor, but Ginsburg chose the second floor suite because it had more light. After a visit from Cecilia Marshall, widow of the late Justice Marshall, Ginsburg said, "Mrs. Marshall came to greet me and said she was so glad I had taken his chambers. I have tremendous admiration for Justice Marshall."[1]

During the 1970s, Justice Thurgood Marshall listened as Ruth Bader Ginsburg argued six cases before the Supreme Court. In each case, he voted in favor of her clients. Now that she had attained a seat on the

Supreme Court, Ginsburg reflected on Marshall's reaction to the struggle for women's equality. She said, "He considered women's rights important and understood better than most the unfairness of discrimination based on birth status, unrelated to ability and achievement."[2] Ginsburg had often been compared to Marshall, and now she sat in the very rooms that he used during his twenty-four year tenure on the bench.

Even though Ginsburg had officially been a Supreme Court Justice since her swearing-in on August 10, 1993, she had not been officially welcomed to the Court. That ceremony took place on October 1, 1993, and included a photography session in the courtroom and another oath of office. In attendance were four hundred guests who witnessed the proceedings and then went to a reception that was held in the conference room.

In addition to the welcoming ceremony, a traditional dinner party was given for each new member of the Court by the other eight Justices and their spouses. It gave all of the Justices an opportunity to get to know each other. They would be working very closely with each other in the months and years ahead.

Ruth Bader Ginsburg has been characterized by some of her friends as a shy and reserved woman who takes her work very seriously. A colleague from her teaching days said, "She can make small talk and be very pleasant. But she prefers to talk about ideas, the law. Her eyes light up, and she interrupts, and she becomes a very animated person."[3]

During sessions of the Supreme Court, the nine Justices take their seats behind the curved bench.

In spite of Ginsburg's serious nature, her husband Martin said after the confirmation, "I think my wife is terrific. And now, so does everyone else."[4] Martin Ginsburg had been his wife's most ardent supporter during all of their thirty-nine years together. When Ruth Bader Ginsburg was being discussed for a possible Supreme Court nomination, Martin Ginsburg was right there pulling for her. He asked some of his wife's colleagues to write letters of support to the President. And Martin Ginsburg presented to the officials who investigated the Supreme Court nominee precise tax and financial records so that there would be no controversy in regard to the Ginsburgs' income. In response to her husband's unflagging support, Ruth Bader Ginsburg said:

> Some men are less confident about themselves than my husband is! You have to have a lot of self-security in order to regard your life's partner as someone who is truly equal, not somehow less important.[5]

She also said about Martin Ginsburg:

> I have had the good fortune to share life with a partner truly extraordinary for his generation, a man who believed at age 18 when we met and who believes today that a woman's work, whether at home or on the job, is as important as a man's.[6]

In their marriage, Ruth and Martin Ginsburg had shared equally in the duties of home and professional life.

They each had successful careers and lived very comfortably in the Watergate Apartments in Washington, D.C. On weekends, the couple enjoyed playing golf and visiting friends and traveled to Europe each year to attend various legal conferences.

The Ginsburg's adult children have successful careers of their own. Jane Ginsburg is an attorney and teaches at Columbia University Law School. She is married to George T. Spera, Jr., and the couple has two children, Clara and Paul. James Ginsburg, a graduate of the University of Chicago, owns a company that produces classical music recordings.

While Jane and James were growing up, their parents often took them to the symphony and opera. Ruth Bader Ginsburg's love of the opera led her to put on a white powdered wig and appear as an extra with The Washington Opera in January 1994. Along with fellow Supreme Court Justice Antonin Scalia, she remained on stage for nearly an hour and a half. The two Justices did not speak any lines or sing but were part of a play within a play. Their characters were directed to watch and react to the activity that was taking place on stage, so that the audience saw not only the opera but also the reactions of the extras. For her operatic stage debut, Ginsburg put a feather in the white wig that she wore.

In addition to her love of music, Ginsburg also likes to watch old movies and read. She was asked during her confirmation hearings what kinds of books she reads for

Ruth Bader Ginsburg poses with the other Supreme Court Justices for their official 1993 photograph. (Left to right: Sandra Day O'Connor, Clarence Thomas, Harry A. Blackmun, Anthony M. Kennedy, Chief Justice William H. Rehnquist, David Hackett Souter, John Paul Stevens, Ruth Bader Ginsburg, and Antonin Scalia).

enjoyment. Ginsburg replied that she reads mostly fiction during her spare time because she must read so much factual material in connection with her work. She also said that her husband Martin often selects her books because he knows what she likes.[7]

Ruth Ginsburg often addressed the concept of what was considered men's work and women's work. She said:

> Remember that I came from a world where women were protected out of everything. Protected out of being lawyers, out of being engineers, out of being bartenders. Women couldn't work in certain occupations that were regarded as dangerous but also happened to pay better.[8]

In 1973 she stood before the all-male Supreme Court Justices and quoted a nineteenth-century feminist, Sara Grimke, who said, "I ask no favor for my sex. All I ask of our brethren is that they take their feet off our necks."[9] Women wanted to be given the opportunity to prove that they were capable of doing the same jobs as men.

Ginsburg appeared to rally around those who attempted to reverse some of the gender stereotypes. One of her law clerks, David Post, was the principal caretaker for his children. He had also clerked for Ginsburg when she was an appeals court judge. For years he had tried to arrange his schedule so that he would be available for his young son and daughter. His efforts were unusual in a world where most men go to work and leave child-rearing to the women.

Ruth Bader Ginsburg (left) poses with daughter Jane Ginsburg and son-in-law George Spera.

When David Post asked for flexible work hours, Ginsburg quickly agreed. She said about her clerk:

> He is a great role model, he is tremendously capable, but he doesn't need to be in my chambers when he has to pick Sam up at school. He can work at home. You show by example, and he's going to be a wonderful example for my colleagues.[10]

One of Ginsburg's former clerks said, "On a personal level, Ginsburg has a passionate commitment to family and friends and values her clerks as another family."[11] Daughter Jane concurred when she said about her mother, "She's very struck by what happens to people. She would say to me, We're not only talking about grand abstract principles, we're talking about *people*."[12] In spite of her serious exterior and unwavering demand for excellence, Ginsburg also seemed to possess a warm and caring nature that was widely recognized by those who were closest to her.

Justice Ginsburg

Shortly before the Court's fall 1993 term began, Ruth Bader Ginsburg went to New York City to accept an award from the American Bar Association. After the ceremony, she answered questions that were asked by several of the reporters who were in attendance. One reporter commented on the fact that now there would be two women on the Supreme Court. Ginsburg said:

> I do think that being the second woman is wonderful, because it is a sign that being a woman in a place of importance is no longer extraordinary. It will become more and more common.[1]

Justices Sandra Day O'Connor and Ruth Bader Ginsburg had a lot in common. They were nearly the same age and had similar experiences after graduating from law school. In spite of excellent academic records, both had difficulty finding employment. Each overcame career obstacles that would have stopped many others and eventually reached the pinnacle of the legal profession, the Supreme Court.

After the appointment of Ruth Bader Ginsburg, Justice O'Connor praised her future colleague for her work on behalf of women's rights. O'Connor added that in spite of the advances that women had made they "still have the primary responsibility for children and housekeeping, spending twice as much time on those chores than their professional husbands."[2]

Ruth Ginsburg echoed many of those same sentiments when she said, "Motherhood has been praised to the skies, but the greatest praise men can give to that role is for them to share in doing it. That's my dream for the next generation."[3] With the addition of Justice Ginsburg to the Supreme Court, there would now be two female perspectives among the nine Justices.

Late in 1993, Ruth Bader Ginsburg and Jane Ginsburg attended a program in Washington, D.C., that featured a panel entitled "Mothers and Daughters in Law." On the panel were women who were considered to be early advocates for women's and civil rights and their daughters, who were also attorneys. One of the mothers, Marion Phillips, related that she had been one of only two women in her law school class. When she first began working, she tried to appear less attractive to draw attention away from her gender. In spite of her attempts, she was usually called "sweetheart" and "girlie" by her colleagues instead of "attorney" or "counselor."[4]

During the panel discussion, Jane Ginsburg said that her mother's attention to detail was evident when she checked her daughter's homework and made her do it over and over until it was perfect. "Her day off was not my favorite," said Jane. She later took advantage of her mother's editorial expertise and sent her first law-review article home to be corrected.[5]

Ruth Bader Ginsburg had a great deal of paperwork to do in connection with her job. There were briefs to be read and opinions to be written. Occasionally, when she ran out of time at the office, she took some of it along with her to work on during free moments. One time she was observed at a restaurant with her husband, quietly pouring over a stack of briefs while they waited for friends. On another occasion, someone saw her in a movie theater using a small flashlight to read with during the coming attractions. After the incident in the theater made the Washington newspapers, Ginsburg was amazed that her sometimes compulsive work habits would be interesting enough to attract the attention of the press. She reacted to the article by saying, "Now this is news!"[6]

As Justice Ginsburg worked her way through the more than one thousand petitions that had accumulated over the summer, her first day on the Supreme Court bench quickly approached. When the first session in October arrived, the nine Justices entered the courtroom, and each shook hands with the other eight. That tradition was initiated in the 1800s by Chief Justice Melville Fuller to "remind the Justices that, despite their differences, all members of the Court shared a unity of purpose."[7] The handshake was also performed when the Justices met in conference.

Justice Ginsburg, the newest member of the Court, took her place in a seat on the far left side of the bench, facing the courtroom. Chief Justice William Rehnquist occupied the middle chair, and seniority determined the placement of the other Justices. To the right of the Chief Justice sat the senior Associate Justice and to the left of Rehnquist sat the next most senior member. The positions alternated, with the most junior members of the Court occupying the seats at either end of the table. When the Justices were in the conference room, the junior member would speak last, take messages, send for documents, and open the door for the other Justices.

On her first day as a Supreme Court Justice, Ruth Bader Ginsburg added a triangle of white cloth, called a rabat, to the neckline of her black robe. During the following weeks, Justice Sandra Day O'Connor wore a ruffled rabat, and Justice Anthony Kennedy temporarily wore bright scarves draped around a neck brace that he had to wear following surgery. In an atmosphere that is heavily governed by tradition, the addition of neckwear was a rather bold statement.

The newest Supreme Court Justices occupy the seats at the ends of the bench.

Instead of spending her first weeks on the Court as a silent observer and student of the process, Justice Ginsburg jumped right into the proceedings. In most of the cases that appear on the Supreme Court docket, each side has thirty minutes for argument. The Justices are able to ask questions from the bench, and Ginsburg began right away to fire questions at the attorneys that stood before the Court. On her first day as a Justice, Ruth Bader Ginsburg asked seventeen questions during the first hour of the session.

Justice Antonin Scalia was also known as an aggressive questioner, and after Ginsburg joined the bench, many of the other Justices also seemed to speak up more often. Only Justices Harry Blackmun and Clarence Thomas remained quiet as usual. Before long, the lawyers who tried to argue their cases began to complain that they did not have enough time to present their material. Until 1970, each side had one hour for argument. (In the last century there was no time limit, so some cases lasted for several days.)

In the present Court, time is watched very carefully, and when it is used up, all argument ceases. Some have suggested that extra time should be given when it is needed, so that all questions can be answered to the satisfaction of those present. Experienced advocate, Carter Phillips, agrees that thirty minutes is not adequate, especially with the increased questioning from the bench.[8]

Washington attorney Erwin Griswold is among those who have been critical of Justice Ruth Bader Ginsburg's extensive questioning technique. He said, "She has spent 12 years on a court with three judges, and now she is on a court with nine. I would hope someone would get word to her that she should take less time."[9] At one point during the 1993–94 session, Ginsburg interrupted a question asked by Justice Sandra Day O'Connor. "Excuse me!" said O'Connor. "Just let me finish." The following day, Ginsburg interrupted Justice Anthony Kennedy as he questioned an attorney.[10]

Some view her aggressive participation in a positive light. *Legal Times*, a weekly publication devoted to issues of law, named Ginsburg a "winner" when it reported:

> Making the most impressive high-court debut in memory, Justice Ruth Bader Ginsburg gave a clinic on how to hit the ground running. . . . Ginsburg provided a strong reminder of what happens when a president sends an extremely well-qualified candidate to the bench.[11]

12

From the Bench

More than two hundred attorneys appear before the Supreme Court in a typical year. Their cases cover a wide range of topics that the nine Justices must carefully deliberate. Some have a far-reaching effect on American life. Others affect fewer people, but they are still important to those who are involved. One case that came before the Court during Justice Ruth Bader Ginsburg's first term concerned the issue of capital punishment.

In 1972, in the decision of *Furman* v. *Georgia,* the Supreme Court returned the opinion that the death penalty should be struck down because it could be classified under the cruel and unusual punishment clause of the Eighth Amendment to the Constitution. There were more than six hundred inmates on death row in the United States at that time, and all plans for their executions were halted. Then, in 1976, in the decision of *Gregg* v. *Georgia*, the Supreme Court reversed its former decision and agreed to permit capital punishment. Once again criminals were sent to death row, and plans were made for their executions.

The issue that came before the Court in 1994 concerned the possibility of an alternative punishment to the death penalty. The Supreme Court Justices ruled that juries must be informed about the option of life in prison, without the possibility of parole, when deciding death penalty cases in the states that permit executions. There are nearly three thousand convicts on death row in U.S. prisons who might be affected by the new ruling concerning capital punishment.

Another less serious case, *Campbell* v. *Acuff-Rose Music, Inc.* (1994), came before the Court during Justice Ginsburg's first term. It concerned the music industry and the rap group 2 Live Crew. Acuff-Rose Music Company held the copyright to the late Roy Orbison's song "Oh, Pretty Woman." 2 Live Crew wanted to do a rap parody of the song, but they were denied permission to use the lyrics by the music company.

The rap group went ahead and recorded the song and included it on an album that they released called "As Clean as They Wanna Be." Acuff-Rose sued 2 Live Crew, and the case was tried in a Tennessee court. In the Tennessee case, the court ruled in favor of 2 Live Crew and said that the group had not violated the copyright laws.

Acuff-Rose Music Company appealed the ruling to a higher court, where the decision was reversed. Since there were now two opposing rulings, the case was once again appealed, this time to the Supreme Court. After hearing all of the testimony, the nine Justices unanimously agreed that 2 Live Crew had not infringed on the copyright laws when they recorded the parody of "Oh, Pretty Woman." Justice David Souter wrote for the Court and ". . . held that a careful satirist can borrow from his victim without permission."[1] He went on to say that 2 Live Crew had altered the beat and changed most of the lyrics from the original song and had not infringed on the Orbison copyright.[2]

One-third of the cases that the Supreme Court heard during the 1993–94 term dealt with the issue of sexual harassment. In relation to the cases, the Court had to try and define just what sexual harassment on the job included. Extensive debate took place concerning proper terminology and whether the term "reasonable woman" or "reasonable person" should be used and how the employer's behavior could be measured.

Ginsburg, a lifelong advocate for women's rights, was very involved in the arguments and questioned the attorneys at length. She finally commented that sexual harassment might be found if ". . . one sex has to put up with something that the other sex doesn't have to put up with." Ginsburg asked, "Is it really more complex? The terms and conditions of employment are not equal if one person is being called names and the other isn't."[3]

Women had made great strides in their struggle for equality since the days in the 1970s when Ruth Bader Ginsburg argued the first gender discrimination cases before the Supreme Court. Without her groundbreaking work, sexual discrimination might never have been brought into the light of day. Many women were no longer willing to suffer humiliation at the hands of their employers and had the courage to voice their complaints. Unfortunately, there were still many areas of life in which women took a backseat to men.

In 1992, women made up 57.8 percent of the civilian workforce in the United States.[4] In spite of the fact that women outnumbered men in the workplace, they continued to be paid less. The 1991 median income for females was $20,553 and for men, $29,421.[5] The earnings gap had been in existence since women first entered the job market, as had the problems of sexual discrimination and harassment.

It was for those continuing inequalities that Ruth Bader Ginsburg still supported passage of the Equal Rights Amendment. During her confirmation hearings, she said about ratification of the ERA:

> I regard it as a highly desirable measure and for this principal reason: We do have an Equal Protection clause phrased broadly enough to cover the same territory, but it is historic fact that the framers of that clause—the framers of the 14th Amendment—were not thinking about the legal equality of men and women[6]

In her own life, Ruth Bader Ginsburg rose above many deterrents that might have stopped another. She managed to be both a successful mother and attorney. Her respected work as a professor, a litigator, and a judge led to her ultimate appointment to the Supreme Court. During her first year on the Supreme Court, the Justices issued only eighty-two opinions, the smallest number since 1955.

The 1994–95 term brought one significant change to the bench. Justice Stephen Bryer replaced retiring Justice Harry Blackmun, a member of the Court since 1970. Ruth Bader Ginsburg would no longer be the most junior member of the Court. She would move to the last seat on the right of the Chief Justice so that Bryer could take the last seat on the left of the bench.

Among the cases that the Supreme Court heard early in the 1994–95 term was one that concerned the R. J. Reynolds Tobacco Company. The tobacco giant was sued in 1991 by Janet Mangini, an attorney in the San Francisco area. Mangini read that the tobacco company's cartoon symbol, Joe Camel, was as well known to children as Mickey Mouse. Mangini's suit asked for a ban on the symbol and a campaign, financed by R. J. Reynolds, that advertised to children that smoking "is not cool." Among her arguments in support of the ban were statistics from the American Medical Association. They said that the sale of Camel cigarettes to teenagers rose from $6 million when Joe Camel first appeared in 1988, to $476 million in 1992.[7]

Mangini's suit was thrown out by a California state court. She appealed the decision, and the case was reinstated by the California Supreme Court. R. J. Reynolds sought to prevent the case from being heard and appealed to the Supreme Court to have the lower court ruling upheld. The Supreme Court then refused to prevent the lawsuit from being heard in Court. The fate of the Joe Camel symbol will ultimately be decided after all of the evidence for both sides is presented in a California court.

Another case that the Justices had to consider involved drug testing in an Oregon school district. A seventh-grade student was prevented from playing football for his school when he refused to submit to a drug test. The Vernonia school board has passed a measure in 1989 that called for drug tests for all student athletes. The boy's parents sued the district because they thought that the drug policy violated their son's Constitutional right to be free from unreasonable searches.[8]

After a federal judge ruled against the family, the Ninth U.S. Circuit Court of Appeals reversed the judge's decision. It said that the drug test requirement violated the Constitution. The school district then appealed the case to the United States Supreme Court. The Justices will have to weigh the evidence and decide whether school districts have the right to require drug tests under the provisions of the Constitution. After much deliberation, the Court will hand down a ruling by July 1995.

For many years into the future, Ruth Bader Ginsburg will take her place on the bench and hear the important cases that come before the highest Court. The work is intricate and demanding, but she is very well prepared to offer her opinions. Many of the cases require a great deal of research and study before a decision can be reached. Ginsburg will no doubt be prepared for each case just as she has been prepared for each challenge during her life.

Ruth Bader Ginsburg's early work on behalf of women made history along with her appointment as the second woman ever to serve on the United States Supreme Court. During the nominating ceremony in the White House Rose Garden, President Clinton put it best when he said:

> If as I believe the measure of a person's values can but be measured by examining the life the person lives, then Judge Ginsburg's values are the very ones that represent the very best in America.[9]

Indeed, Ruth Bader Ginsburg's past actions speak volumes about her ability and compassion. She faced tragedy and near tragedy in her personal life, along with many challenges in her professional life. As each obstacle arose, Ruth Bader Ginsburg met it head-on with skill and determination. Along with her husband, Martin

Ruth Bader Ginsburg (second from right) poses with her family, son James, daughter Jane, son-in-law George Spera, and husband Martin.

Ginsburg, she successfully raised two children while waging a battle for gender equality. As she enters the Supreme Court building, Ruth Bader Ginsburg can look up at the words "Equal Justice Under Law" and know that she contributed a great deal to the realization of that goal.

Chronology

1933—Born to Celia and Nathan Bader on March 15 in Brooklyn, New York.

1934—Sister Marilyn dies of meningitis.

1950—Graduates from high school; Celia Bader dies.

1954—Graduates from Cornell University; marries Martin Ginsburg.

1955—Daughter Jane born on July 21.

1956-1958—Attends Harvard Law School.

1959—Graduates from Columbia Law School; admitted to the state bar of New York.

1959-1961—Clerks for District Court Judge Edmund Palmieri.

1961-1962—Research associate of Columbia University Law School project on international procedure.

1962-1963—Associate director of Columbia University Law School project on international procedure.

1963-1972—Professor at Rutgers University Law School.

1965—Son James born on September 8; writes *Civil Procedure in Sweden* with Anders Bruzelius.

1972-1980—Professor at Columbia University Law School; founds and directs the Women's Rights Project of the American Civil Liberties Union.

1973—Argues and wins first case before the Supreme Court.

1974—Coauthors *Text, Cases, and Materials on Sex-Based Discrimination.*

1980–Judge on the United States Court of Appeals for
-1993   the District of Columbia Circuit.

1993–Nominated to the United States Supreme Court on June 13; confirmed by the Senate on August 3; sworn in as the 107th Justice of the United States Supreme Court.

Chapter Notes

Chapter 1

1. Kermit Hall, ed., *The Oxford Companion to the Supreme Court of the United States* (New York: Oxford University Press, 1992), p. 83.

2. "Clinton Nominates Ginsburg to Supreme Court," *Congressional Quarterly*, June 19, 1993, p. 1599.

3. Ibid.

4. "Justice for Women," *Vogue*, October 1993, p. 392.

5. Henry Reske, "Two Paths for Ginsburg," *ABA Journal*, August 1993, p. 16.

6. *Congressional Quarterly*, June 19, 1993, p. 1600.

7. Ibid.

8. Ibid.

9. Ibid.

Chapter 2

1. David Margolick, "Trial by Adversity Shapes Jurist's Outlook," *The New York Times*, June 25, 1993, p. A19.

2. Letter from Justice Ginsburg to the author, July 1, 1994.

3. "The Second Woman Justice," *ABA Journal*, October 1993, p. 42.

4. Lynn Gilbert and Gaylen Moore, *Particular Passions* (New York: Potter, 1981), p. 156.

5. Margolick, p. A19.

Chapter 3

1. Margaret Carlson, "The Law According to Ruth," *Time*, June 28, 1993, p. 38.

2. David Margolick, "Trial by Adversity Shapes Jurist's Outlook," *The New York Times*, June 24, 1993, p. A19.

3. Ibid.

4. Elinor Swiger, *Women Lawyers at Work* (New York: Messner, 1978), p. 55.

5. "Justice for Women," *Vogue*, October 1993, p. 473.

6. Swiger, p. 55.

7. Ibid., p. 58.

8. "The Second Woman Justice," *ABA Journal*, October 1993, p. 41.

9. Margolick, p. A19.

10. Lynn Gilbert and Gaylen Moore, *Particular Passions* (New York: Potter, 1981), p. 158.

11. "Ruth Ginsburg: Carving a Career Path Through Male-Dominated Legal World," *Congressional Quarterly*, July 17, 1993, p. 1877.

Chapter 4

1. David Margolick, "Trial by Adversity Shapes Jurist's Outlook," *The New York Times*, June 25, 1993, p. A19.

2. Lynn Gilbert and Gaylen Moore, *Particular Passions* (New York: Potter, 1981), p. 159.

3. Ibid.

4. Elinor Swiger, *Women Lawyers at Work* (New York: Messner, 1978), p. 60.

5. Bill Hewitt, "Feeling Supreme," *People*, June 28, 1993, p. 50.

6. Swiger, p. 64.

7. *Statistical Abstract of the United States* (Washington, D.C.: U.S. Bureau of the Census, 1992).

8. Margolick, p. A19.

Chapter 5

1. Kermit Hall, ed., *The Oxford Companion to the Supreme Court of the United States* (New York: Oxford University Press, 1992), p. 680.

2. Ibid., p. 589.

3. Michael Parrish, *Anxious Decades* (New York: Norton, 1992), p. 136.

4. "Ginsburg Adroit, Amiable but Avoids Specifics," *Congressional Quarterly,* July 24, 1993, p. 1986.

5. Parrish, p. 141.

6. *The 1994 Information Please Almanac* (New York: Houghton Mifflin, 1994), p. 56, and *Information Plus,* 1992, p. 24.

7. Lynn Gilbert and Gaylen Moore, *Particular Passions* (New York: Potter, 1981), p. 153.

8. Eric Foner, ed., *The Reader's Companion to American History* (Boston: Houghton Mifflin, 1991), p. 356.

9. Gilbert and Moore, p. 155.

Chapter 6

1. Kermit Hall, ed., *The Oxford Companion to the Supreme Court of the United States* (New York: Oxford University Press, 1992), p. 713.

2. "First No to Sex Bias," *Time,* December 6, 1971, p. 71.

3. Lynn Gilbert and Gaylen Moore, *Particular Passions* (New York: Potter, 1981), p. 156.

4. Ruth B. Cowan, "Women's Rights Through Litigation," *Columbia Human Rights Law Review,* Spring–Summer 1976, p. 389.

5. Cowan, p. 389.

6. Ibid., p. 394.

7. "Sex Equality: Impact of a Key Decision," *U.S. News & World Report,* May 28, 1973, p. 69.

8. Ibid.

9. Elinor Swiger, *Women Lawyers at Work* (New York: Messner, 1978), p. 52.

10. Cowan, p. 394.

11. "The Remarkable Rise of Ruth Bader Ginsburg . . ." *Congressional Quarterly Researcher*, September 17, 1993, p. 822.

12. Stephanie B. Goldberg, "Heady ACLU Years," *ABA Journal*, August 1993, p. 18.

13. "Justice for Women," *Vogue*, October 1993, p. 473.

Chapter 7

1. Henry Reske, "Two Paths for Ginsburg," *ABA Journal*, August 1993, p. 21.

2. "Clinton's Choice of Ginsburg Signals Moderation." *Congressional Quarterly*, June 19, 1993, p. 1570.

3. Margaret Carlson, "The Law According to Ruth," *Time*, June 28, 1993, p. 40.

4. "Ginsburg Tailored Radical Arguments to Fit Mainstream," *Legal Times*, June 21, 1993, p. 16.

5. "The Second Woman Justice," *ABA Journal*, October 1993, p. 43.

6. "Ginsburg Tailored Radical Arguments to Fit Mainstream," p. 13.

7. Reske, p. 20.

Chapter 8

1. "Ginsburg Adroit, Amiable but Avoids Specifics," *Congressional Quarterly*, July 24, 1993, p. 1982.

2. Ibid.

3. Ibid., p. 1987.

4. "Ginsburg Marches Past Hearings on Near-Certain Path to Court," *Congressional Quarterly*, July 24, 1993, p. 1958.

5. "Ginsburg Adroit, Amiable, but Avoids Specifics," p. 1986.

6. Ibid.

7. "Ginsburg Marches Past Hearings on Near-Certain Path to Court," p. 1957.

8. "Ginsburg Adroit, Amiable, but Avoids Specifics," p. 1989.

9. Ibid., p. 1988.

Chapter 9

1. Robert Wagman, *The Supreme Court: A Citizen's Guide* (New York: Pharos Books, 1993), p. 285.

2. "The Court's Growing Caseload," *Congressional Quarterly Researcher*, September 17, 1993, p. 825.

3. *The Supreme Court of the United States* (manual) (Washington, D.C.: The Supreme Court Historical Society, 1993), p. 9.

4. Ibid., p. 3.

Chapter 10

1. "Ginsburg Offers Early Reaction to New Post," *Legal Times*, September 27, 1993, p. 10.

2. Letter from Justice Ginsburg to the author, July 1, 1994.

3. "Ginsburg Tailored Radical Arguments to Fit Mainstream," *Legal Times*, June 21, 1993, p. 16.

4. "Justice for Women," *Vogue*, October 1993, p. 473.

5. Angela Hunt, "Women Right Now," *Glamour*, October 1993, p. 117.

6. "Ginsburg Adroit, Amiable but Avoids Specifics," *Congressional Quarterly*, July 24, 1993, p. 1982.

7. Ibid., p. 1988.

8. Hunt, p. 117.

9. Aaron Epstein, "All Eyes to be on Women in High Courts," *Austin American-Statesman*, October 3, 1993, p. H1.

10. "Ginsburg Offers Early Reaction to New Post," p. 14.

11. Henry Reske, "Two Paths for Ginsburg," *ABA Journal,* August 1993, p. 20.

12. "Justice for Women," p. 472.

Chapter 11

1. "The Second Woman Justice," *ABA Journal,* October 1993, p. 43.

2. "Women in a Cage," *Houston Chronicle,* October 29, 1993 p. A2.

3. Angela Hunt, "Women Right Now," *Glamour,* October 1993, p. 117.

4. Sarah Hodder, "Like Mother, Like Daughter," *Legal Times,* November 1, 1993, p. 58.

5. Ibid.

6. Tony Mauro, "Those Justices Just Won't Stop Talking," *Legal Times,* December 6, 1993, p. 11.

7. Kermit Hall, ed., *The Oxford Companion to the Supreme Court of the United States* (New York: Oxford University Press, 1992), p. 989.

8. Mauro, p. 10.

9. Ibid.

10. "Rude Ruth," *Newsweek,* April 11, 1994, p. 6.

11. "Winner," *Legal Times,* December 27, 1993, p. 5.

Chapter 12

1. David Van Biema, "Parodies Regained," *Time,* March 21, 1994, p. 46.

2. David Stewart, "Rock Around the Docket," *ABA Journal,* May 1994, p. 52.

3. Linda Greenhouse, "Talk Puts Ginsburg Fore of Court Debates," *The New York Times,* October 14, 1993, p. A1.

4. *The 1994 Information Please Almanac* (New York: Houghton Mifflin, 1994), p. 56.

5. Ibid., p. 59.

6. "In Her Words: Ginsburg on Abortion, Confirmation Process, Equal Rights," *Congressional Quarterly*, June 19, 1993, p. 1573.

7. Richard Curelli, "Setback for Joe Camel," *Houston Post*, November 11, 1994, p. A1.

8. Student Drug Testing Due High Court Review," *Houston Post*, November 29, 1994, p. A6.

9. "Clinton Nominates Ginsburg to Supreme Court," *Congressional Quarterly*, June 19, 1993, p. 1600.

Further Reading

Carlson, Margaret. "The Law According to Ruth." *Time*, June 28, 1993, pp. 38–40.

Fry, William R., and Roy Hoopes. *Legal Careers and the Legal System*. Springfield, N.J.: Enslow Publishers, Inc., 1988.

Gay, Kathlyn. *The New Power of Women in Politics*. Springfield, N.J.: Enslow Publishers, Inc., 1994.

Hall, Kermit, ed. *The Oxford Companion to the Supreme Court of the United States*. New York: Oxford University Press, 1992.

Hewitt, Bill. "Feeling Supreme." *People*, June 28, 1993, pp. 49–50.

"Justice for Women." *Vogue*, October 1993, p. 392ff.

Lindop, Edmund. *Birth of the Constitution*. Springfield, N.J.: Enslow Publishers, Inc., 1987.

"Ruth Bader Ginsburg." In *Current Biography Yearbook, 1994*. New York: H.W. Wilson Co., 1994.

Wagman, Robert. *The Supreme Court: A Citizen's Guide*. New York: Pharos Books, 1993.

Weiss, Ann. *The Supreme Court*. Springfield, N.J.: Enslow Publishers, Inc., 1987.

Index

128